The Adventures of Bertie MacButton

Bertie and the Snow Dragon

Written by Maureen Gill-Beedie

Illustrated by Jeannie Duncanson

This book is dedicated to my late parents,

George and Isobel Beedie,

who nurtured my love of reading.

First Printed in 2022

Copyright © Maureen Gill-Beedie 2022

Illustrated by Jeannie Duncanson

ISBN: 978-1-7396677-1-9 (Paperback 2nd edition, 2023)

The Adventures of Bertie MacButton

www.macbutton-books.com

mo@bertiemacbutton.co.uk

This Bertie MacButton
Adventure belongs to:

_____

I hope you enjoy it

Love Bertie

Bertie MacButton is furry and sweet,

A magical dog, I want you to meet,

He lives with his family, Ruby and Mum,

Together they all have adventures and fun.

Bertie sees creatures, unseen by you,

Magical animals, hidden from view,

He does things, that no other dog can,

Bertie, is from the MacButton Clan.

When he paws at the ground, and stares at the

sky, Bertie MacButton is able to fly!

Mum said, "Ruby I have a surprise,"

"A surprise," said Ruby with saucer sized eyes,

"Lottie's party's tomorrow — you'll have lots

of fun,"

"A party?" said Ruby, "Can Bertie come?"

"Oh Yes," said mum,

"But he'll need to dress up,"

He'd worn the same bow-tie, since he

was a pup!

"Let's make him a new one, that would be fun,"

Oh yes, thought Bertie, a red tartan one.

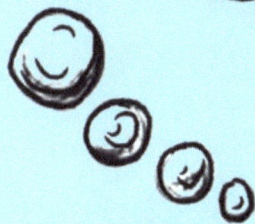

The day of the party, it was time to go,

But Bertie was worried, he could see

lots of snow,

Mum said, "Oh dear, we'll need to stay warm,

The sky is heavy, and we may have a storm."

We'll just have to walk, we can't take the car,

Lottie lives on a farm, but it isn't too far,

Ruby and mum, got dressed in warm clothes,

Bertie's thick fur meant he didn't need those.

When they were ready,

off they did go,

Ruby and Bertie played

in the snow.

The snow kept on falling,

it covered the ground.

Faster and faster, it made

not a sound.

They walked really quickly, then mum said

"No!"

"We can't go any further, there's just

too much snow,"

Bertie was worried, looking up at the sky,

Then Suzie the Snow Dragon let out a cry.

Nobody saw him, he made not a sound,

He looked at the sky and pawed at the ground,

Up into the air, little Bertie flew,

He'd gone to see Suzie, she'd know what to do.

"Are you lost little Bertie?"

She cried from above,

"Yes," said Bertie,
"I'm with the people I love,"

"I'll help you Bertie, we'll find a way.

People are important"

He heard Suzie say.

"Don't worry" said Suzie,

"They can sit right up here,"

A dragon, thought Bertie might fill

them with fear,

"I won't hurt them," said Suzie,

"I have gentle wings,"

Bertie knew people were scared of

such things.

Suzie the Snow Dragon thought

For a while,

Then her big friendly face started to smile,

"Don't worry Bertie we won't leave

them behind,"

Bertie was happy he knew Suzie was kind.

She took a big breath, her face it did glow,

And Suzie blew flames, right through the snow,

She melted a path and showed Bertie the way,

Bertie thanked Suzie,

she'd saved the day!

Bertie found mum, and Ruby too,

He woofed, and showed them just what to do,

They followed the path that Suzie had made,

Soon they were home, and at

home they stayed!

Bertie has a secret, and we all know,

It wasn't just Bertie, who helped in the snow,

T'was a dragon, that saved them in the end,

And Bertie was glad, that she was his friend.

www.ingramcontent.com/pod-product-compliance
Lightning Source LLC
LaVergne TN
LVHW072120070426
835511LV00002B/45